Researching Brewery
and Publican
Ancestors

SECOND EDITION

Simon Fowler

THE FAMILY HISTORY PARTNERSHIP

Published by
The Family History Partnership
PO Box 502 Bury
Lancashire BL8 9EP

First published by FFHS (Publications) Ltd. 2003
Second edition 2009

Copyright © Simon Fowler

ISBN: 978 1 906280 12 3

Printed and bound by
Information Press, Southfield Road, Eynsham
Oxford OX29 4JB

Contents

Preface

The inn has long been regarded as one of England's glories. Indeed the public house is largely a phenomenon of the British Isles. In Ireland Inns have become a major tourist attraction, with fake 'Irish pubs' now found from Tokyo to Tallinn.

Inns, public houses, whatever you care to call them, have been around since medieval times and probably earlier. For centuries they were the major source of entertainment outside the home and the church. Even today with the vast range of leisure choices at our disposal pub-going is still popular. There can be few readers who have not ventured inside a public house for a drink or meal. Indeed some people, like your author, have spent some of the happiest times of their lives in pubs.

Much of the charm of the public house depends on the landlord and their staff. A beautifully appointed pub may suffer from an uninterested publican and surly staff. Conversely a scruffy and seemingly down-at-heel establishment may offer a warm welcome and fine ale. Pubs are much more than just the landlord and his wife, most employ bar maids, cellarmen and cleaners. In the larger coaching inns of the eighteenth century there were innumerable staff engaged in looking after patrons and their customers.

And pubs wouldn't be pubs without beer, once upon a time usually made on the premises, but today likely to have been shipped hundreds of miles. The relationship between breweries and pubs has always been a close one: brewers depend on pubs to sell beer for them, while publicans needed beer to slake their customers' thirsts and may also depend on brewers financially for cheap loans. Breweries, too, were labour intensive, employing many different workers in the brewhouse, bottling plant or on drays delivering the finished product.

Of course, both brewery workers and publicans left descendants, who now want to find out more about their ancestors. This booklet is an attempt to help people who discover that they have innkeepers or brewers in their family. Documents on the brewery trade can be difficult to find and interpret. There was no clear career structure as relatively few people made innkeeping their career of choice unless their family was already involved in the trade. Most seemed to have drifted into running pubs for a few years, perhaps combining it with another job, and when having failed to make a go of it — for although it looks simple to customers, running a successful and profitable pub is tricky — they moved on elsewhere. On the other hand there were families who ran pubs, passing on skills from generation to generation.

Breweries however, were different. Many people spent their working life with a particular firm; with several brewers having had a paternalistic reputation for looking after their staff, paying higher than normal wages (albeit for very long hours) and providing facilities such as a bar on-site.

This book comprises two sections. The first is a brief survey about the changing nature of brewing, the pub and the people who worked there, which might help if you are trying to discover more about your ancestor and the places they worked in. The second part offers advice about the records and where you can find them. There's also a glossary of terms you may come across in the course of your research, a short bibliography and list of relevant websites.

This second edition has been thoroughly revised to take advantage of resources now available online and other changes in the archival world.

I'm grateful for the help of Jeff Sechiari of the Brewery History Society and Steve Williams of the Pub History Society, who looked over a number of chapters in the book. Thanks also to Bob Boyd and Terry Walsh of the Family History Partnership for publishing the new edition.

PART ONE

Introduction

THE PUBLIC HOUSE

The public house as we know it today is really an invention of the eighteenth century. Before then there were alehouses that sold beer brewed on the premises often by women, known as alewives or brewsters. More salubrious were inns, much larger establishments, which provided food, stabling for horses, and a variety of dining and meeting rooms. They often became the centre of local society and economic life. A census of inns and taverns taken in 1577 showed that there were just under 20,000 licensed establishments in England and Wales — or roughly one to every 187 of the population. The current ratio is in the region of 1:1050.

The eighteenth and nineteenth centuries saw a massive rebuilding of pubs in reaction to changing tastes as well as the opening of new establishments to meet new demand in industrial and suburban areas. Tobias Smollett noted in 1752 that London pubs: "were the haunts of idleness, fraud and rapine, and the seminaries of drunkenness, debauchery, extravagance, and every vice incident to human nature."

By the end of the eighteenth century pubs were being bought up by breweries with the object of selling their products to a fairly captive audience. By 1820, perhaps half the pubs in London were tied to a brewer, by the end of the century this had risen to well over 90 per cent. Even twenty years ago it was still difficult to find a genuine freehouse in the metropolis.

Until the mid-nineteenth century the only feature that distinguished a pub from a private house was the sign over the door. The building might be divided into several drinking areas. Drinks were brought to the customers by the staff (normally the landlord or his wife); there was no bar in the modern sense. What was then called a bar was a separate private room, which approximated to the reception room and office of a modern hotel. The first bar counter in the modern sense may have been built at the railway refreshment rooms on Swindon station by Isambard Kingdom Brunel in order to process the large number of passengers who all wanted serving at the same time.

The arrival of gas lighting in the 1820s and 1830s led to the refurbishment of many pubs and the construction of new establishments. According to Charles Dickens the fashion for these new 'gin palaces' as they were called: "rushed to every part of town, knocking down all the old public houses and depositing splendid mansions, stone balustrades, rosewood fittings, immense lamps and illustrated clocks at the corner of every street." At the same time there was an explosion in the number of pubs as Wellington's Beer Act of 1830 allowed anybody to buy a licence for two guineas. In 1831, 30,000 new beer houses alone were opened.

It wasn't until 1869 that licensing of pubs by magistrates was reintroduced. Local authorities and magistrates, egged on by the temperance lobby, sought to close pubs as a way of reducing drunkenness among the working classes. In the 1870s a huge proportion of the budget of working class families - in some cases up to a quarter - was spent on drink, causing great misery and ruin for many. As a result, a quarter of all pubs mainly in working class areas, were closed before the First World War. In addition increasing restrictions were placed on pubs, particularly with regard to opening and closing hours and pub games that involved an element of gambling.

The numbers of people visiting pubs also began to decline with the arrival of other leisure attractions, especially those laid on by churches, such as choirs, outings and Sunday schools. After the First World War came the cinema and the radio, followed by television after the Second World War. By the 1930s beer consumption was only 40 per cent of what it had been sixty years previously. It is little wonder that the numbers of licensed premises declined rapidly.

	Total number of licensees	Population per pub
1831	82,480	168
1851	95,484	188
1871	112,884	201
1891	105,006	276
1911	90,586	398
1931	77,049	517
1951	73,421	595
1971	77,878	626
2007	57,000	1,052

Many brewers reacted to the late-Victorian restrictions by building a second generation of gin palaces, full of etched glass and fine decoration to attract responsible drinkers. The Philharmonic in Liverpool and the Princess Louise, near Holborn station, in London are fine surviving examples of this style. After the First World War, what became known as the model pub movement saw the building of larger establishments in new residential areas and along new arterial roads. These often provided a variety of attractions from bowling greens to restaurants — often referred to as being built in a 'brewer's tudor' architectural style.

The movement to provide more welcoming pubs really took off after the Second World War. People now had a far greater choice of leisure activities (including, of course, family history), so the attractions of drinking sour beer in smoky pubs waned. The brewers and publicans have fought back by providing food, television and a variety of drinks, to attract women as well as men of all social classes. The changes have been so great that the traditional 'back-street boozer' or country inn where our ancestors slaked their thirst has all but disappeared. Over 30 pubs a week are now closing. Breweries and now more often giant pub owning companies (known as 'pubcos'), find the land a pub stands on is worth more than the trade generated by the pub itself.

The people

Over the centuries hundreds of thousands of people have run pubs. Indeed it stills remains an ambition for many a drinker, although few realise how hard the work is. There are no clear rules on how to run a public house, or how people became publicans, alewives or innkeepers, but the following suggestions may help you in your search.

- A number of publicans were former sportsmen or servants (such as butlers and footmen) who often saw a pub as a way of providing for their retirement.
- Many children followed their parents into running pubs. Girls started as barmaids or working in the kitchen, while boys became potboys or ostlers.
- It was extremely common for publicans, particularly in smaller establishments, to work only part-time, so combining running a pub with other work, such as plumbing or carpentry. During the day running the pub was left in the hands of the wife and other members of the family.
- A number of women also ran pubs, often taking over on the death of their husband or father.

Pub terminology

Your ancestor may have undertaken one or more of these tasks:

The publican Sometimes known as the landlord, licensee, licensed victualler, 'the gaffer', 'gov'nor' or 'mine host'. It is he (surprisingly often she) who holds the licence to run the pub and it is his job to ensure the financial success of the premises. Many licensees are tenants of a brewery, that is, they run the pub on an agreement with the brewery which owns it, and pay the brewery an agreed amount every year in rent. Over the past thirty years or so salaried managers, put in by the company, have begun to run an increasing number of pubs.

Barmaids Female bar staff were often the wives or daughters of publicans, although by the end of the nineteenth century barmaids were being hired in the larger and more popular establishments. Victorian sensibilities ensured that barmaids only worked in the more expensive saloon or lounge bars, where a better class of customer was served. Pay was low and hours long, although it was the custom for accommodation and meals to be included.

Barmen Tended to be young men. They were better paid than barmaids, although hours were as long. Most only remained as barmen for a few years, before seeking other work.

Cellarmen Were employed to look after the barrels of beer. They tended to be found in the larger or busier establishments. Elsewhere the publican or barstaff usually managed the cellars.

Ostlers Were men and boys who looked after the horses in coaching inns. This was important work as dozens of coaches might pass through an inn everyday.

Potmen or Potboys Were originally employed to keep pewter drinking mugs clean and shiny. As glassware replaced pewter during the nineteenth century, these people were increasingly used to collect glasses from tables in the bar and to act as general servants. They were less well paid than the barstaff.

THE BREWERY

Until the arrival of tea and coffee in the second half of the seventeenth century, beer was drunk by all sections of society. Because the water used in brewing had been boiled it was much safer to drink than pure water, and the nutrients contained in the brew were a valuable supplement to an otherwise meagre diet. The ale drunk was much darker, stronger and sweeter than we are used to today. Surviving accounts for the convent at Syon in Middlesex in 1371 show that nuns were given seven gallons of ale a week, that is eight pints a day. This was probably weaker small beer: the customary drink of women and children. Even so many of our ancestors must have spent their lives in an alcoholic stupor.

Hops, which are both a preservative and add a pleasing bitterness, were only introduced from the Continent in the early fifteenth century. It took many years for this new drink, called beer, to supplant the older ale. As late as 1542, Andrew Boorde in his *Dietary of Health* complained that beer: "troubles drinkers with colic, and the stone and the strangulation... yet it doth make a man fat and doth inflate the belly."

Until the eighteenth century, brewing was a small-scale business undertaken at taverns, monasteries and farms, often by women known as alewives or brewsters. The first commercial brewers appeared during the seventeenth century in London. Samuel Pepys was partial to a beer produced by a Mr Bide in the East End. In 1667, he noted in his diary as he returned to Mile End with William Penn from the country and called in at the Rose and Crown "a good place for Alderman Bide's Ale". The Faversham brewer, Shepherd Neame, founded in 1698, is probably Britain's oldest continuous brewer, although this is disputed by the Blue Anchor Brewery in Helston, Cornwall.

The eighteenth century saw a rapid growth in the size of breweries. Many of the firms, which were household names a generation ago, were founded then. In London, Thrale started in 1729, followed by Whitbread in 1742. In Burton-on-Trent Worthington (1744) and Bass (1777) were established. George's was founded at Bristol in 1788, Ind at Romford in 1779 and in Ireland Guinness was established in Dublin in 1759. By 1781, the six largest firms in London were producing 80,000 barrels of beer a year. The biggest brewers were perhaps the largest enterprises in operation at the time: only the Admiralty was bigger.

By the mid-eighteenth century the Staffordshire town of Burton-on-Trent was on the way to becoming Britain's premium centre for brewing. Here the water was found to be particularly suited for brewing pale ale, most notably India Pale Ale (IPA) which was sparkling and pleasantly bitter. It also helped that Burton was on a river which allowed the easy transportation of beer to Hull and other ports. By 1800 90,000 barrels were being exported each year from the town. Even today water is 'burtonised' by the addition of gypsum salts, by brewers to make it like the water, or liquor in brewers' terminology, found in Burton.

The liquor in London, however, was more suited to the production of dark beers such as porter and stout. Porter was the favourite tipple of London's working classes for nearly two centuries. A French writer in 1726 described it as being "a thick and strong beverage and the effect it produces in excess is the same as that of wine." It had to be matured for several months before it could be sent to pubs. Huge vats were constructed to store the beer. Inevitably disaster struck. In 1814 one of the vats of the Horseshoe Brewery in Tottenham Court Road burst its hoops, and the resulting flood of beer caused the demolition of three neighbouring houses and the deaths of eight people.

The larger brewers expanded by buying pubs, which were then tied to sell their beers, or by selling beer through the free trade. Bottled Bass Ale, for example, was widely available across Britain and much further afield. Most brewers, however, brewed only for a farm or a single pub. In 1840, there were 50,000 brewers. This number declined rapidly during the Victorian period. In 1880 there were half that number and by 1900 just over 3,000 survived. There are several reasons for this decline. For households and pubs it became cheaper to buy beer than to make it themselves, particularly as taxation increasingly discriminated against small producers. Larger brewers bought up smaller breweries for the pubs that they owned. Lastly, brewers faced a growing temperance movement which called for restrictions on the manufacture and sale of drink and often provided sober alternates to the pub.

The decline in the number of breweries continued during the twentieth century, leading to the emergence of a few giant breweries with a scattering of middle sized regional brewers, and smaller local firms who somehow escaped being swallowed up by their larger competitors. Many of the breweries which were taken over or closed down were extremely badly run. They had produced undrinkable beer which was served in unattractive and poorly maintained pubs. One such brewery was Offiler's of

Derby, which Anthony Avis said had one of the "sleepiest breweries I had encountered, even in an era of comatose management". The company was "feudal, dormant and without energy, sense of purpose or direction", although it has to be said that the beer is still remembered by local drinkers with pleasure.

Since the first edition of this book was published this trend has continued: the largest breweries have been swallowed up by multinational companies and two 'super-regionals' (Greene King and Marstons) have absorbed a number of smaller breweries. In Leicestershire, for example, in 1880 there were 40 brewers, this had fallen to seven in 1941, and just two (Everards and Hoskins) in 1981. Since then there has been a steady growth in very small brewers trading (known as micro-breweries). There are now about 400 breweries, compared with 100 or so twenty years ago. In Leicestershire there are now ten breweries, although only Everards is of any size.

The people

Until the onset of mass mechanisation after the Second World War breweries employed large numbers of people, particularly in work such as maintenance of equipment, bottling, coopering (making the barrels) and distribution of the finished product, as well as the clerical and administrative side. The writer Blanchard Jerrold and the artist Gustave Doré visited a London brewery in 1871, and noted that against the great towers and barrels the workers "looked like flies." In Doré's engravings these dark anonymous shapes tend to the duties like religious votaries. There are fitful gleams illuminating the activities of the small figures in vast enclosed spaces.

In the smaller breweries everybody would be expected to lend a hand when the need demanded. Small country brewers might only employ a few men, but the very largest, such as Bass in Burton, employed over 2,700 men who brewed well over a million barrels of beer a year. Fifteen packed trains took Bass's annual staff outing to Liverpool, New Brighton and the Isle of Man in July 1904.

The work could be seasonal, with people being taken on at

times when the brewery was busy and laid off when things were quiet. Every winter in Burton large numbers of agricultural workers, known locally as 'Norkies', came from East Anglia to work in the town's maltings. Despite the intensive nature of the work it was much sought after because it was far better paid than the subsistence wages paid on farms.

The larger companies in particular provided reasonable working conditions for their employees. Free beer was one bonus which was much appreciated, but the thoughtful worker might also take advantage of savings clubs, and inexpensive housing provided by the brewery. The Stag Brewery in Mortlake built a small estate - Watney Road - to house its workers during the 1920s. There might have also been a canteen. Anthony Avis who worked at the Fountain Brewery in Bradford during the 1940s, remembered its canteen presided over by the formidable Mrs Teagle the cook: "the food was solid, traditional, filling, always hot and full of cholesterol!" (which had not then been invented)!

As a result breweries had few problems in recruiting staff. It was not uncommon for several generations to work with the company. In London staff were often recruited from the provinces. In his research for *London Labour and London Life* the social investigator, Charles Booth was told in the 1890s by several brewers that: "countrymen are steadier and healthier and not so well acquainted with the distractions and ideas of town life as cockneys."

Family tradition is probably the best way of identifying ancestors who were brewery workers. Although you should remember that over time the ancestor who washed the bottles or maintained the mash tun, may have grown in retelling to have been the head brewer who eloped with the chairman's daughter! You are likely to be able to locate brewery ancestors in the censuses, although you will then have the problem of finding out which firm they worked for. An alternative source may be street or trade directories.

Brewery terminology

Some of the people who worked at breweries were:

Directors and chairmen	With a team of accountants they were responsible for the management of the brewery. The chairmen often had a reputation for eccentricity and for many, until the 1950s at least, the brewery solely existed to keep them and their families in the lifestyle to which they had become accustomed. They can be identified from shareholders' guides and trade publications.
Head Brewer and assistants	They were responsible for the production of the beer and ensuring that the quality was maintained. Many head brewers spent their whole career with a single company and rarely had any formal scientific or technical training. They too can often be identified from trade directories.
Coopers	Made and repaired the wooden casks (barrels) in which beer was stored and distributed to pubs. An experienced cooper could make up to four casks a day.
Draymen	To many people they were the public face of the brewery delivering beer to local pubs. Indeed a small number of breweries still maintain a small stable of horses and drays for publicity purposes. In late-Victorian times, according to Charles Booth they were "the tired sleepy men who may be met at almost any hour of the day or of a summer night, driving out their full dray or returning with their empty barrels. One of them, either drayman or trouncer [his assistant], is usually to be seen asleep among the casks which make up the load."

PART TWO

The Records

This section looks at most of the common sources which you can use to find out about publicans and brewery workers.

Licences

From 1552 onwards, anyone who wanted to sell ale had to apply for a licence at the Quarter Sessions or the Petty Sessions. In addition alehouse keepers had to declare that they would not keep a 'disorderly house' and would prohibit games of bowls, dice, football and tennis. These declarations were called recognizances or bonds. Although the requirements have changed over the years, landlords still have to get a licence, renewed yearly. Until recently they were issued by magistrates, meeting in the annual brewster session, and could be revoked if they felt that the individual had been running a disorderly pub. This power has now been transferred to local councils.

In 1617 the need to obtain a licence was extended to inns. In addition between 1570 and 1792 licences could be obtained directly from the Crown (from 1757 the Stamp Office) rather than from local magistrates, although few records now survive. The system was overhauled in 1828 with a new Alehouses Act that provided a framework for granting licences to sell beer, wine and spirits and for regulating inns.

Records of licences can generally be found in Quarter and Petty Session records at local record offices. You should look out for registers of recognizances and licences granted to licensed victuallers. Few records however survive before the middle of the eighteenth century, but an Act of 1753 enforced the keeping of such registers, so most counties have some material from then onwards. Again the system fell into abeyance, particularly after 1828, but detailed registers have been kept since 1871.

The most detailed registers give the name of the licensee, the parish in which he lived, the inn sign (i.e. name of the pub), and the names of occupations of two guarantors who vouched for the applicant's probity. However, you are more likely to find just the names of individuals and possibly the parish they came from, with no indication of which pub he ran.

Within the records there may also be correspondence, copies of bonds and notes that might contain other information. Many licensing records may only refer to the pub name rather than the licensee, so it is important to know exactly which pub an ancestor ran.

The most useful introduction to these records is Jeremy Gibson's *Victuallers' Licences* 3rd ed., Family History Partnership (2009). The Access to Archives project has put catalogues of all Quarter Sessions records online at **www.nationalarchives.gov. uk/a2a,** so you can see what survives and where.

Records of breweries
Some breweries keep their own records, but a number have been deposited at local record offices. Because of the great changes taking place in the brewing industry at present it is not always clear where the records of the larger brewers are located. The Brewery History Society is keeping an eye on the situation to ensure the brewery archives are maintained by their new owners or transferred to the appropriate archival repository. The National Register of Archives, maintained by The National Archives, may also be able to help. Another useful, if now rather dated, source is Lesley Richmond and Alison Turton, *The Brewing Industry: a Guide to the Historical Records* (Manchester University Press, 1990).

A number of breweries have published histories, which vary from academic works to publicity brochures. A good recent example is Brian Glover's *Brains 125 years* (Brain's, 2007) about the iconic Glamorgan brewery. More unusual is Helen Osborn, *In and Around London: a History of Young's Pubs* (Young's, 1991). Of particular interest is the Whitbread Library, a series of illustrated books about the brewery, the craftsmen it employed and some of the pubs owned, which were published in the late 1940s.

Unfortunately almost all books of this type can be hard to track down. The best place to start is probably the local history library in the area where the brewery was located. Paul Travis of Beer-Inn Print (see page 46 for address) has a number for sale, or for second-hand books you can try **www.abebooks.co.uk**, or **www.alibris.co.uk** or **www.ebay.co.uk**.

Surviving records vary dramatically from brewery to brewery. Those which are most likely to exist relate to the purchase and sale of their pubs. They survive because these were legal documents and were likely to have been referred to fairly often by the brewery staff. Other records you might find are minute books, inventories of pub furniture and equipment taken when an establishment changed hands, wage books for brewery staff, applications for employment and occasionally house journals.

It can also be difficult to work out which brewery originally owned a pub. If you don't already know this, it is worth trying to track down an old photograph of the pub which may include the sign indicating the name of brewery which once owned it. Local studies libraries (see p. 30) often have large, and well indexed collections of local photos. There may also be newspaper articles containing reports about the change of ownership. If the pub is still trading, the locals and the landlord may be able to help.

Once you have found the right brewery, their records may tell you from whom the pub was bought or when the land it was built on was acquired. Estate records are usually held in alphabetical order by premises, and may include title deeds, mortgages, maps and plans, pub lists and books containing lease and conveyance details. In addition there may also be records of beer sold (known as barrelage in the trade) by the pub, although here too the records are arranged by property rather than by the publican.

OTHER RECORD SOURCES

Apprenticeship records

Many young men were apprenticed to brewers, although it can be difficult to find evidence of this, as the indentures (that is the agreement between brewer and apprentice) rarely survive. However there are two places to look for indentures in the eighteenth century. Firstly there are records of the stamp tax paid on indentures between 1710 and 1811, which are at The National Archives (TNA) in series IR 1. Secondly, many years ago the Society of Genealogists (SoG) indexed these records between 1710 and 1774: copies of these indexes are at both TNA and the SoG (there are plans to extend the indexes after 1774). In addition the Society has a number of original apprentice indentures, while others may be found at local record offices. Apprenticeship records for the London livery guilds of Brewers and Innholders are with the Guildhall Library (see under Guilds on p. 24) with indexes at **www.britishorigins.com**.

Biographical sources

Successful brewers have often become respected members of society, entering politics or even in rare cases becoming ennobled. Several generations of Samuel Whitbreads in the eighteenth century were both brewers and radical politicians. Many members of the Bass family became MPs and Michael Bass was raised to the peerage in 1880, unsurprisingly as Lord Burton. If you suspect that you are descended from a well-known brewing family it is worth checking the *Oxford Dictionary of National Biography* (DNB), *Who was Who,* and other more specialist dictionaries of biography to see whether there are entries. The SoG has a large collection of this kind of material. Incidentally the *Oxford DNB* and *Who was Who* is available online at every public library.

Buildings

Breweries, maltings and public houses all occupied (or occupy) distinctive buildings which were designed and built round the functions which would take place therein. The classic Victorian brewery, for example, occupied what was known as a tower brewery. The movement of liquids through the brewing vessels could easily be achieved if the main ingredients – malt and water – were winched and pumped to the top of a tower so that gravity could provide much of the energy needed during the brewing process. Fine examples survive in everyday use in Lewes, East Sussex and Hook Norton, Oxfordshire.

Maltings occupied extremely long buildings where barley was spread out in huge rooms and germinated for malt. Few now survive in their original forms, but the buildings may have been turned into flats, office complexes or arts centres.

Pubs come in all shapes and sizes from what were clearly once cottages, to purpose built medieval coaching inns and 1930s estate pubs. Interiors and exteriors were, and are, regularly altered to meet changing fashions and the brewer's whims. Indeed of the 55,000 or so pubs open today fewer than 500 have interiors which have remained largely unaltered. These are noted in the Campaign for Real Ale's National Inventory (see p. 36).

There are many records about the architectural features and aesthetic merits of individual buildings. The National Monuments Record in Swindon (address on p. 33) has much of interest. The search engine at **www.heritagegateway.org.uk** will trawl through various databases to come up with photographs and descriptions of listed buildings and those of particular architectural merit.

An excellent website **www.buildinghistory.org** offers guidance on researching old buildings (particularly houses), although there is nothing specifically about breweries or public houses. The best introduction for beginners to house history (and by default pubs and, to a lesser extent, breweries) is probably Anthony Adolph's *Collins Guide to House History* (HarperCollins, 2006).

Census

Census returns survive for the period between 1841 and 1901. The 1911 census will be released during 2009 (more details at **www.1911census.co.uk**).

Census records are all online at **www.ancestry.co.uk**. In addition **www.findmypast.com** and **www.britishorigins.com** have most years available (with plans to do the others). The 1881 census is available for free at **www.familysearch.org** and the 1901 census (with an excellent index) at **www.1901census.nationalarchives.gov.uk**.

As occupations of individuals are described in the census enumerators' books it is fairly easy to pick out publicans and brewery workers. For 1881 the work has been done for you: there is an excellent online list of pubs and publicans at **www.1881pubs.com**. The numbers identified in the Registrar General's reports on 1841 and 1901 censuses were as follows:

	1841	1901	1901M	1901F
Maltsters	7,965	9,607		
Brewers	9,357	27,919	27,822	97
Innkeepers etc	58,875	99,915	75,895	24,020

M = Male   F = Female

If a licensee ran a pub part-time the other occupation may also be noted, such as 'publican and plumber'. Other members of the household listed in the returns were likely to have been involved with the pub in one way or another. The name of the pub is also often included, together with its address. If not you may be able to identify it from a local street or trade directory.

It can be much more difficult to identify which brewery a particular person worked, especially in places like London and Burton where there were a number of breweries in operation. A very rough guideline may be to assume, at least initially, that the ancestor worked at the brewery closest to where he lived, although of course there is no guarantee that this was the case.

Company records

Most modern companies are incorporated with limited liability or joint stock, so that the shareholders and the directors only face minimal financial penalties if the company becomes bankrupt. Before 1844 this arrangement was available only to companies through an Act of Parliament. New legislation in 1844 said that any company could have limited liability provided they regis-tered and submitted annual returns to Companies House. Although the Act has subsequently been amended many times this is still the basic procedure today. Many small family-run, or private companies (including many breweries), however, did not bother to register.

The National Archives has registration documents for com-panies, formed in England and Wales, which are no longer trad-ing, such as memoranda of agreement outlining the purpose for which the company was formed and lists of directors and share-holders. Records for companies formed between 1844 and 1860 are in series BT 41. Records however have been kept for only a sample of companies dissolved after 1860 – initially a large sam-ple, but now details of only five per cent of modern companies are kept. They are arranged in company number order, which can be supplied by Companies House, although TNA has a few indexes. The equivalent for Scotland is at the National Archives of Scotland (NAS). Companies House, in both England and Wales and Scotland, can supply this information over the phone (0870 3333636), but you have to know the exact name of the company. More information can be obtained at the website **www.companies-house.gov.uk** or by contacting:

Companies House	Companies House (Scotland)
Crown Way	37 Castle Terrace
Cardiff	Edinburgh
CF14 3UZ	EH1 2EB

What TNA (or to a lesser extent the NAS) does not have are the administrative records created by the companies, which may include minutes of boards of directors and any committees, finan-cial records, publicity material and staff records. There is no legal requirement for records to be kept for more than a certain period, as a result relatively few records survive. It is always worth con-tacting companies still in business to see whether they can help. The National Register of Archives (NRA, maintained by TNA) should be able to tell you whether any records survive in local record offices and where they may be found.

A useful guide to these records is Eric Probert's, *Company and Business Records for Family Historians* (FFHS, 1994), which is currently out of print although local family history societies may have a copy. A more detailed book is John Orbell, *Tracing the History of a Business* (Gower, 1987). The National Archives produces several useful readers' guides describing the major sources, which can be downloaded at **www.nationalarchives.gov.uk/catalogue**.

Directories

Directories list all trades people, local notables and householders. They were most important in the late nineteenth century, although they date from the late eighteenth century. Breweries and pubs will be listed and the publican normally named. In addition there may well be advertisements for breweries and the larger inns, particularly in tourist areas. As directories were published every year or so, it is possible to work out roughly the length of time a person ran a pub and, perhaps, his career moving from pub to pub.

The Guildhall Library (details on p. 32) holds the largest national collection of directories — although the Society of Genealogists (details on p. 33) also has a sizeable holding, mainly street directories. Local libraries and record offices should have some directories for their area and others have been published by companies such as S&N **www.genealogysupplies.com**. A number for the 1850s, 1890s and 1910s are also available online at **www.historicdirectories.org**.

There are a number of specific trade directories for the brewing industry, including:

The Brewers' Directory and Licensed Victuallers' Guide, 1871 (Walker & Co, London, [1871.]); *The Post Office Directory of the Brewers and Maltsters* (Kelly & Co, London, 1877); *Kelly's Directory of Wine and Spirit Trades, with which are included Brewers and Maltsters* (Kelly & Co) various years from 1882; *The Operative Brewers' Directory, 1927-1928* (Brewers' Guild, London, 1928), continued as *the Incorporated Brewers' Directory* in 1934-1935 and subsequent years.

The British Library Newspaper Library has sets and they may also be available at specialist brewing libraries (see p. 34).

The Brewery History Society has published a list of almost every British brewery in existence between 1890 and 2004 in *A Century of British Brewers, 1890-2004* (3rd edition, BHS, 2005). The Society is also publishing much more detailed lists of brewers, county by county (see p. 36). Manfred Friedrich's *Gazetteer of the Breweries of the British Isles* (1982) is a very detailed guide to brewers of the late-Victorian period: all the more remarkable as the author apparently spoke no English! A few volumes have been reprinted by the BHS: at present Cambridgeshire and Durham are available.

Guilds

During the medieval period urban trades often organised themselves into guilds in order to restrict entrants, provide training for members and generally protect their interests. In London, the Worshipful Guild of Brewers received its charter from the Crown in 1437. Its history is told in Mia Ball's *The Worshipful Company of Brewers: a short history* (Hutchinson, 1977). Most records of the Company seem to have been lost when its hall was bombed during the Blitz. Some apprenticeship and other records are at the Guildhall Library (address on p. 32). More details are given in a free leaflet produced by the Library *Sources for Tracing Apprenticeship and Membership in City Livery Companies and Related Organisations*, which can also be downloaded from their website **www.ihrinfo.ac.uk/gh/livdet.html**. From them Cliff Webb has compiled an index of London Apprentices who were members of the *Brewers' Company 1685-1800* (Vol 1, SoG, 1996). This includes a list of the apprentices to the company, including name of master, often name of father and home parish and gives the date when the apprenticeship started.

Coopers played an important role in breweries making and repairing barrels. The Worshipful Company of Coopers received its charter in 1501. Surviving apprenticeship and membership records are at the Guildhall Library, including apprenticeship and freedom records between 1529-1571 and 1689-1949 and lists of freemen 1667-1971.

The Worshipful Company of Innholders, for publicans, received its charter in 1514. A brief history of the Company can be found on its website **www.innholders.co.uk**. Fuller details are given in Oliver Warner's *A History of the Innholders' Company* ((London, 1962). Some apprenticeship and other records are at the Guildhall Library. Again Cliff Webb has produced a list of apprentices in his *Innholders' Company 1642-1643, 1654-1670, 1673-1800* (SoG, 1998) in Volume 17 of the London Apprentices' series of books for the Society of Genealogists.

Some records for brewers' guilds outside London can occasionally be found at local record offices. In particular the records of the Chester Brewer's Company, between 1606 and 1966, are with the Cheshire and Chester Record Office.

Insurance records

Many brewers and publicans insured their premises, particularly the larger and busier establishments, against fire and other damage. Industrial accidents were particularly common in breweries. If you know that your ancestor's pub had been burnt down, it is worth checking insurance records. The largest collection, which is particularly strong for the London area, is at the Guildhall Library. Unfortunately the records are not easy to use unless you know the policy number and the company with which the property was insured.

However, detailed indexes to the Sun Fire Office policy registers between 1808 and 1839 (at the Guildhall Library) are available on the Access to Archives website at **www.nationalarchives.gov.uk/a2a.** The indexes are particularly useful because Sun was the largest insurance company at the time and include details of many claims from brewers and publicans. More information can be found at **www.history.ac.uk/gh/ sun.htm.**

Land records

Even quite small public houses in rural areas are likely to have a plot of land attached. Descriptions of this land will appear in tithe and enclosure maps and accompanying documents, which are roughly for the period between 1750 and 1850. Sets of these records can be found at TNA and at local record offices. Valuation Office returns, between 1911 and 1915, (at TNA) describe individual pubs and the land they occupied in both urban and rural areas, although they are difficult to use. Ordnance Survey and fire insurance maps will show breweries and pubs and the land they occupied in towns — sets of these maps are normally found in local record offices. Local record offices may also have records about the sale of properties.

There may also be records at the Land Registry particularly for modern sales. A useful guide to using these records is at **www.pubhistory.freeserve.co.uk/phs/landregistry.htm**. The Land Registry's websites are **www.landregistry.gov.uk** and **www.landregisteronline.gov.uk**.

Newspapers

Newspapers are an important — and under-used resource for finding information about brewers, publicans and the pubs they ran. There may be stories about changes at local breweries and the activities of staff, the departure of long-serving landlords, events which took place in local pubs, such as darts tournaments and annual dinners, court cases involving local brewers (perhaps for the adulteration of beer) and publicans, and the activities of prominent local brewers and publicans perhaps within the Licensed Victualler's Association or in charity work. It is also worth looking out for notices about the sale of inns and breweries and advertisements from breweries describing the beers they sold and how much they cost. Pubs also sometimes advertised their facilities.

Local record offices and local studies libraries are likely to have newspapers for their areas. The national collection of newspapers is at the British Library Newspaper Library (details on p. 31). The British Library is also busy digitising many nineteenth century newspaper collections, although unfortunately at present the results are only available to academics but presumably they will be made more widely available in due course.

The archives of several national newspapers are now available online: *The Times* (and *Sunday Times*) is at **http://archive.timesonline.co.uk**

The Guardian (and *Observer*) **http://archive.guardian.co.uk**; and *The Scotsman* **http://archive.scotsman.com**. In each case searches are free, but you may have to pay to view the results. A quick search of *The Times* came up with nearly 5,000 references to the Bass brewery.

The best guide to newspapers is Jeremy Gibson's, *Local Newspapers 1750-1920* (2nd edition, Federation of Family History Societies, 2002).

With the exception of *The Times*, *Guardian* and *Scotsman* few local newspapers are indexed, although it is always worth asking at your local studies library whether there is an index for the period in which you are interested. You may have to go through many months' worth of issues before you find anything of interest. Many local studies libraries have good collections going back for more than a hundred years. Breweries, pubs, publicans and the activities which took place in them are all likely to appear here.

The British Library Newspaper Library also has copies of the various trade papers and journals published for the industry (see appendix 1 on page 37). Most were extremely short lived but contain many stories about individual brewers and publicans, and stories about developments and challenges facing the trade. The longest running and most important of these is the *Morning Advertiser*, which was founded in 1801. For many years it was read in the trade largely for its racing tips!

Personal papers

Very few brewers or publicans have left personal papers behind. If you are lucky, they may include letters or perhaps account books. This material may either have been deposited with the local record office or is, perhaps, still in the family's possession. The National Register of Archives (see under TNA, p. 33) will be able to tell you whether any records survive for your ancestor.

Photographs

Many local studies libraries have collections of old photographs of streets and street scenes which may include your ancestor's pub or the brewery where he worked. My local library, for example, has a fine collection of photographs of Richmond taken a century ago, which show most of the local pubs.

English Heritage's National Monument's Register in Swindon has a number of collections of old photographs of buildings, worth checking (see p. 33). A recent accession is a collection of slides of pubs formerly owned by Allied Breweries (which took over Ind Coope, Friary Meux and Halls among other breweries). They include interior and exterior views, with some slides showing promotional material. This collection dates from 1960 to 1990 and covers the whole country although London is dominant.

The National Archives has several large collections of photographs. Those taken between 1870 and 1912 and submitted to Stationer's Hall for copyright purposes are in COPY 1. An index is available as part of the online catalogue at **www.nationalarchives.gov.uk/catalogue**. A collection of street scenes taken in the 1930s by the Dixon Scott postcard company is in INF 9. Neither are primarily about pubs (or breweries) but you may strike lucky.

Ratebooks

Rates have long been levied on property, normally of the reasonably well-to-do. Before the twentieth century separate highway and poor rates were levied, but they were usually collected together, and details recorded in rate books, which can now be found in record offices. They list the householder, landlord if appropriate, and rate levied with a brief description of the premises. Pubs will be included, although it can sometimes be difficult to identify individual properties

Wills

About ten per cent of people made wills before 1900. Innkeepers are likely to be among this number as they often had property to bequeath. Wills are useful because they list family members and give an impression of wealth and possessions held.

Before 1858 wills were administered by a complicated system of ecclesiastical courts. They are found at various record offices depending on how rich the person making the will was. Many for Northern England are with the Borthwick Institute at the University of York, Heslington, York YO10 5DD,

www.york.ac.uk/inst/bihr. The Prerogative Court of Canterbury however was the largest and most important court. Its records are at The National Archives and can be downloaded from the Documents Online service for £3.50 per will at **www.nationalarchives.gov.uk/documentsonline**. The site also includes an index to names and occupations, including 2,739 brewers, 565 publicans and 1,428 innkeepers.

Wills proved after 11 January 1858 are held by the Principal Probate Registry, First Avenue House, 44-49 High Holborn, London WC1V 6NP. They have easy to use surname indexes arranged by year in which probate was granted. Copies cost £5 each (2009 price).There are plans to make these records available online.

Useful Addresses

Most original documents can be found in one of three places: a county record office, a local studies library or a national repository. Details of archives can be found at **www.nationalarchives.gov.uk/archon** and local studies libraries at **www.familia.org.uk**. Alternatively their holdings are briefly described in Janet Foster and Julia Sheppard, *British Archives: a Guide to Archive Resources in the United Kingdom* (3rd edition, Palgrave, 2001) — every reference library should have a copy.

Every county has a county record office: a few cities, such as Southampton or Coventry, also have a city archive as well. These record offices hold material created both by local government, such as rate books, quarter sessions records or council minutes, and unofficial material donated by individuals, companies or clubs, which may include such things as land and house deeds, account books and photographs.

It is important to ring before-hand to book a seat - as most record offices have very cramped reading areas. They should also be able to give you a rough idea whether they have the records you are interested in.

Local studies libraries are the poor relations of the archive world, mainly because they are neither quite an archive nor really a library but contain elements of both. They are likely to have a comprehensive collection of books about the locality, including street directories. Their greatest asset is often a comprehensively indexed collection of press cuttings from local, and sometimes national, newspapers going back to before the First World War. They may also have some original documents, such as Poor Law records or personal papers, but they are usually not the first place to consult original material.

Each local record office has a different system of managing its records, although most follow the same principles of archive administration. Documents are kept together by collection, rather than rearranged by subject as happens in a library. This can be frustrating if you are researching a topic, as you may have to search a number of sources to find what you want. A number of repositories have electronic catalogues, notably those at The National Archives, which can identify documents in a large number of places on the same subject. The catalogues are also usually available on the internet.

Access to Archives (A2A) **www.nationalarchives.gov.uk/nra** provides much the same service for local record offices in England. A2A is extremely easy to use, although it is not comprehensive. However you are unlikely to be able to track down an individual, as the catalogues only record the item description, rather than describe the contents.

Many local record offices and local studies libraries still rely on old-fashioned card indexes arranged by subject. There's usually a heading for the 'public houses' or perhaps others for 'brewers' or 'industry'.

In addition a number of record offices, particularly The National Archives, produce useful introductory leaflets on aspects of the records. Many are now available online.

British Library
96 Euston Road, London NW1 2DB; Tel: 020 7412 7000
www.bl.uk
The British Library is Britain's national library. To get access you have to have a reader's ticket and demonstrate why you need to use the library's collections, although access restrictions have significantly eased in recent years. The library catalogue is available online. It includes the vast majority of books published in the British Isles. It is a useful way to check what books have been published about breweries or pubs in your area.

It should noted that the British Library (at St. Pancreas) holds all London, as well as other newspapers up to 1801. Other British national newspapers and local newspapers are held at: Newspaper Library, The British Library, Colindale Avenue, London NW9 5HE.

Tel: 020 7412 7353.
Guildhall Library
Aldermanbury, London. EC2P 2EJ
Tel. 020 7332 1863
www.ihrinfo.ac.uk/gh
The Library holds much relating to the City of London including
most of the surviving records of guilds and insurance companies,
and a large collection of street and trade directories.

The National Archives
Ruskin Avenue, Kew, Richmond, Surrey TW9 4DU
Tel. 020-8392 5200
www.nationalarchives.gov.uk
The National Archives (TNA) is the national archives of the
United Kingdom and England. Access is free and you do not need
to make an appointment. However you will need to get a reader's
ticket, so don't forget to bring two forms of identity.

For breweries the best place to look is probably among the various series of records related to joint stock or limited liability companies from 1844. However it should be remembered that most
breweries were run by an individual or family and may never
have been registered as a company with limited liability. Also of
interest are records of bankrupts and bankruptcy (also useful for
publicans), which are described in two free readers' guides
Bankrupts and Insolvent Debtors, 1710-1869 and *Bankruptcy Records
after 1869* which can be downloaded from the website or request-
ed by phone. In the Open Reading Room can be found copies of
two Bankrupts Directories held by the Society of Genealogists.
The covering dates for these fiche are 1774-1786, and 1820-1843.

For people interested in publicans, there are lists of inns and
alehouses prepared as possible billets for troops in 1686 and 1756
(series WO 30) and Victuallers' Recognizances (E 180) which were
bonds given by victuallers that they would not kill, dress, or eat
flesh during Lent, keep gaming houses, suffer unlawful games to
be played in their houses, or harbour rogues and vagabonds, etc
between 1578 and 1672.

There are also many records of legal cases in which brewers

and publicans were involved. TNA also holds the records of the Carlisle State Brewery (in series HO 184) and its pubs. The State Management Scheme (as it was known) was in existence from 1916, when the breweries in the city were taken over by the government, until 1971, when the brewery and pubs were sold. In addition there are particularly fine collections of maps and photographs. Its catalogue is online so it is fairly easy to see what records survived for your area.

The National Archives maintains the National Register of Archives and the Access to Archives databases.

National Monuments Record
English Heritage, Kemble Drive, Swindon SN2 2GZ
Tel. 01793 414600
www.english-heritage.org.uk/nmr
The National Monuments Record (NMR) is the public archive of English Heritage with over ten million historic photographs, architectural and archaeological reports, plans and other items related to the historic environment of England. English Heritage is also responsible for the development and management of the national historic environment databases of buildings and sites in England and its territorial waters, together known as the 'Heritage Data Sets' (which include the Listed Buildings dataset), and the development of heritage information partnerships with others.

Society of Genealogists
14 Charterhouse Buildings, Goswell Road, London EC1M 7BA
Tel. 020-7251 8799
www.sog.org.uk
A fee is charged to use the Library for non-members, currently (2009) £4 per hour or £18 per day. The Society's Library is a major resource for family and local historians, with much material that may not be found elsewhere. It has most of the major histories of brewing, a selection of publications produced by the Brewery History Society, and a fair number of local histories and guides to brewing and public houses, all of which can be found using their catalogue (for publicans look under 'Innkeepers') which is now

online via the website.

ARCHIVES WHICH SPECIALISE IN BREWING
OR DRINK RELATED MATERIAL

Birmingham Central Library

Chamberlain Square, Birmingham B3 3HQ

Tel. (0121) 303 4511

www.birmingham.gov.uk/centrallibrary.bcc

Has the extensive archives of the Brewery History Society (see below, a check list is at **www.breweryhistory.com/ archive2.htm)**, as well as records of a number of brewers in the Birmingham area.

Coors Visitor Centre

Horninglow Street, Burton upon Trent, Staffordshire, DE14 1YQ

Tel. 0845 6000598

www.coorsvisitorcentre.co.uk

Formerly the Bass Brewing Museum, the Coors Visitor Centre closed in the summer of 2008, although there is a campaign to turn it into a national museum of brewing. However it still holds the archives for Bass Worthington and the various companies it has taken over since the 1770s. These archives may be deposited shortly with the local record office.

Courage Archives

PO Box 85, Bristol BS99 7BT

moonbeam@easynet.co.uk

Records relating to Courage (now Scottish Courage part of the Scottish and Newcastle Group) and the breweries which it took over since the company was formed in the eighteenth century. The archive is not open to the public, but a free enquiry service operates. Enquiries by email are preferred. Some early Courage material is with the London Metropolitan Archives.

National Brewing Library

Oxford Brookes University, Gipsy Lane, Headington, Oxford OX3 0BP

Tel: (01865) 483156

www.brookes.ac.uk/library/speccoll/brewing.html

With over 3,000 volumes the library has the biggest collection of formal English language brewing related literature in the world. The core of the collection is the unrivalled runs of trade and technical journals from the nineteenth century onwards and treatise and text books on brewing from the eighteenth century to the present day. Other holdings include books on other alcoholic beverages, information on dependent trades (cooperage, engineering, suppliers etc), company histories and house journals, literature on the licensed trade, the temperance movement, alcoholism and health. There is an online catalogue.

Scottish Brewing Archive
Archive Services, 77—87 Dumbarton Road, University of
   Glasgow   G11 6PW
Tel. 0141 330 6079
www.archives.gla.ac.uk/sba/default.html
Has major holdings of Scottish brewers and related records.

Museums and heritage sites
With the closure of the Coors Visitor Centre (formerly the Bass Brewing Museum) in Burton upon Trent, there is no museum dedicated to brewing in Britain. Local museums may have sections devoted to brewing and local breweries, and many surviving breweries have visitor centres and tours which give a flavour of the history of brewing.

   In Newton Abbot, Tuckers Maltings - Britain's only working Victorian Malthouse — offers tours and has a museum. Tuckers Maltings, Teign Road, Osborne Park, Newton Abbot TQ12 4AA; tel: 01626 334734; **www.tuckersmaltings.com**.

   Several other maltings run tours and have small museums attached. In Essex, Great Dunmow Museum is based in an old maltings which has been partly restored. Details from: Great Dunmow Museum, Mill Lane, Great Dunmow CM6 1BG tel: 01371 878979; **www.greatdunmowmaltings.co.uk**

Again there is no museum devoted to the public house, although local museums may have displays. The nearest is probably the Valiant Soldier Museum and Visitor Centre at Buckfastleigh,

Devon. A village inn for two centuries, the Valiant Soldier closed in the 1960s. Furniture, pub artefacts and domestic items remain where they were when the last customer left. Details from:
79 Fore Street Buckfastleigh TQ11 0BS
Tel: 01364 644522
www.devonmuseums.net

The Campaign for Real Ale (CAMRA) maintain a national inventory of historic pub interiors noting the 254 or so pubs where the interiors remain relatively unaltered and whose unique atmosphere is still enjoyed by drinkers. They vary from small, bare-boarded country pubs such as the Red Lion at Ampney St Peter in Gloucestershire, to homely back street locals like the Oxford Bar in Edinburgh (as favoured by Inspector Rebus) and magnificent Victorian gin palaces, such as the Salisbury and the Red Lion in London's West End. These pubs are listed at **www.heritagepubs.org.uk**. CAMRA also publishes a list of these premises and a series of books describing them in more detail:
CAMRA, 230 Hatfield Rd, St Albans AL1 4LW
Tel: 01727 867201
www.camra.org.uk

Societies
There are several societies for enthusiasts and they are normally happy to answer serious and specific enquiries from non-members.

Pub History Society, 15 Hawthorn Rd, Peterborough PE1 4PA
www.pubhistory.freeserve.co.uk/phs/index.htm
Promotes the study and celebrates the history of the pub. It publishes newsletters and journals and organises meetings and study days.

Brewery History Society, Manor Side East, Mill Lane, Byfleet, West Byfleet KT14 7RS
www.breweryhistory.com
The Society publishes a journal, newsletters and a number of guides to defunct breweries. It also organises occasional trips to old breweries of interest.

36

Appendix

A list of trade papers for publicans found at the British Library Newspaper Library.

Place of publication	Title	Date of publication
London	Brewer and Publican	1889-1894
London	Brewer and Wine Merchant and Brewers' Guardian	1907-1947
London	Brewers' Assistant	1881-1886
London	Brewers' Gazette and Wine and Spirits Trade Chronicle	1905-1931
London	Brewers' Guardian	1871-1906
London	Brewers' Guardian	1948 to date
London	Brewers' Journal and Hop and Malt Trades' Review	1867-1967
London	Brewing Trade Review	1886-1972
London	Country Brewers' Gazette, etc	1885-1904
London	Country Brewers' Gazette, Hop and Malt Trades Chronicle	1879-1881
Glasgow	Distillers, Brewers' Spirit and Trade News	1898-1901
Glasgow	Distillers, Brewers' and Spirit Merchants Magazine	1901-1905
Birmingham	Licensed Trade News	1894-1955
London	Licensed Victuallers' Gazette	1958-1966
London	Licensed Victuallers' Gazette and Hotel Courier	1874-1941
London	Licensed Victuallers' Guardian	1869-1887
London	Licensed Victuallers' Mirror	1888-1904
London	Licensing World and Licensed Trade Review	1892-1967
Bradford	Licensee	1912-1915
London	Licensee and Morning Advertiser	1994 to date
London	Morning Advertiser	1801-1965
London	Morning Advertiser and Licensed Restaurateur	1965-1994
Croydon	Publican	1978 to date
Glasgow	Scottish Licensed Trades Guardian	1975 to date
Glasgow	Scottish Licensed Trades	1971 to date

In addition there were a number of short-lived journals, which have not been included here.

Source: BNL Online Catalogue **www.bl.uk/services/reading/newsrrcatalogue.html**

Glossary

The pub trade has a number of special terms, some of which you may come across in the course of your research. The glossary below attempts to provide some definitions:

Ale
Technically an alcoholic drink brewed only with barley, water and yeast. It was sweet and tended to go off very quickly.

Alehouse
Premises with a licence only to sell beer and ale, not wines or spirits. They tended to be small premises, often beginning as the front room of a private house. Almost no pubs today have an ale only licence.

Alewife
A woman in medieval and Tudor times who brewed beer normally for domestic consumption.

Bar
The public drinking area of a public house. Traditionally pubs had two or more such rooms, although over the last forty years most have been knocked into one large area. Bars often had different names, including: bottle and jug (an area set aside for the sale of beer to take home), four-ale bar; ladies bar, lounge, public bar, private bar, saloon, smoke room, tap-room,and vaults.

Barley wine
The strongest beer normally sold in small bottles (known as nips).

Barrel
The normal measure of production of a brewery. A barrel of beer contains 36 gallons (or 288 pints or 163.7 litres).

Barrelage
The amount of beer measured by number of barrels of beer sold by a pub.

Bass Ale
Once Britain's best selling beer, brewed in Burton on Trent since 1777. Its famous trademark — the red triangle — was the first to be registered in Britain. Once upon a time it was also widely available around the world in bottles.

Beer	Basically, ale with hops added to it. Hops were introduced from the continent in the late medieval period as a preservative, although they considerably improved the taste of the beer by making it much less sweet.
Beerhouse	Another term for alehouse.
Bitter	A medium coloured well-hopped beer, which is less sweet than Mild ale and is usually slightly more expensive. This is what you would normally get if you just asked for 'a beer' in a pub.
Brewery	The place where beer is brewed. Many nineteenth century breweries were built in the form of a tower, which allowed the use of gravity to move ingredients at various stages in the brewing process.
Brewster sessions	Another term for licensing sessions, so called because of the numbers of women brewers (brewsters) who used to attend.
Brown ale	Bottled mild.
Cask condition beer	Cask condition beer which finishes its fermentation in the barrel, rather, than being finished at the brewery — usually referred to as real ale today.
Coaching Inn	Large premises which enabled stage coaches to exchange tired horses for fresh ones, about every 20 miles or so during the journey. They also provided meals and refreshment for weary passengers. Because of their size and location in many towns they also became the centre of social and business life, holding balls or acting as a regular meeting place for traders.
Cooper	Made or mended barrels. This was a highly skilled occupation.
Excise Duty	The tax on beer. Traditionally the stronger the beer the greater the tax that was paid on it. In Scotland this led to a general description of beers: 60 shillings (60/-) the weakest (or mild) beer and 90/- the strongest.
Free House	A pub free of any tie to a brewery. During the nineteenth and twentieth centuries the numbers of free houses declined as they fell into the hands of brewery companies.
Hogshead	The largest beer cask size containing 54 gallons (245.5 litres).

Hop	The plant — a perennial climber — whose cones give beer a bitter flavour and improves the period it can be kept. Traditionally British brewers used the male plant, while European brewers preferred the female. Types of hops include Fuggles, Goldings and Styrian.
India Pale Ale (IPA)	A strong bitter, which was matured for a long time to enhance the flavour. This beer was originally exported to British garrisons in India and matured during the long voyage.
Inn	Licensed premises which as well as selling alcoholic beverages also provided meals and accommodation.
Lager	Usually a light coloured beer originally brewed on the continent. Since the 1960s it has become Britain's most popular beer style, although it has been sold in pubs since Victorian times.
License	From Tudor times publicans have been licensed to trade by local magistrates. Publicans running 'unruly houses' were (and are) likely to loose their license.
Licensed victualler	The legal term for a publican.
Licensing sessions	Meetings of magistrates to decide the grant or removal of licenses, although they have had a much wider influence. From the 1870s they actively cut the number of pubs in working class areas in order to discourage drunkenness. More recently they have pressed for the introduction of single bar pubs as a means of controlling trouble. Their functions have recently been taken over by local councils.
Liquor	The term used by brewers to describe water.
Light ale	Bottled bitter.
Maltings	A place where malt is produced from barley (or very occasionally wheat or rye). Grains of barley are steeped in water and then spread out to dry on the maltings floor. When the barley begins to germinate the process is stopped by lightly cooking it in a kiln. Most of the starch in the grains will now have turned to sugar suitable for brewing.

Maltster Was responsible for the malting process. A very skilled job, particularly before thermometers or other equipment was introduced.

Managed house A pub owned by a brewery run by a salaried manager rather than a tenant.

Mild A dark coloured sweet weak beer traditionally a penny or two cheaper than bitter and much favoured by the poorer classes. Sales of mild have fallen considerably and it is now really only drunk in a few areas.

Off licence Shop selling beer and other alcohol for consumption off the premises, i.e. at home. The term was first introduced in 1869.

Old ale A stronger version of mild.

On licence Sale of beer for consumption on the premises i.e. in a pub.

Ostler Initially this was a servant who looked after horses in a coaching inn, but it soon became to mean a general servant.

Pale ale A beer brewed using a pale malt to give a light colour.

Petty sessions A gathering of magistrates to try minor (or petty) crimes.

Porter A style of dark sweetish strong beer popular during the eighteenth century and later. So called because it was supposedly first drunk by porters in London.

Public Bar The bar traditionally frequented by working class men. The furnishings were often sparse, but the beer was sold slightly cheaper than in the saloon bar. Maurice Gorham in *The Local* (Cassell, 1939) noted that: "The Public Bar is the cheapest and most plebeian part of the house, where you pay nothing for decoration, and the mild ale costs fivepence a pint. There are no waiters, no hospital-collecting boxes, no pin-tables (though you will almost certainly find shove ha'penny and darts); you can bring your lunch and eat it without undue comment. In the Public Bar you see more ale [mild] sold than bitter, and pints are less the exception than the rule."

Public House	The term really only came into existence in the eighteenth century originally to describe small drinking places established in private houses. This became extended to include alehouses, taverns and inns.
Quarter Sessions	Quarter sessions were originally meetings of magistrates (JPs) who met together four times a year to dispense justice and discuss the administrative needs of the county, hence the term.
Recognizances	A bond which guaranteed that the individual licensee would run an orderly house.
Saloon	The bar which was often used by women and the more respectable classes. It was better furnished and quieter, although beer cost more than in a public bar. According to Maurice Gorham: "You get (according to the period when the house was last refurbished) the ferns in great brass pots, the bevelled mirrors, the horsehair sofas, the coloured caricature of the landlord done (very cheaply) by a peripatetic artist, the cockatoo in a cage, the open fire, the pin-tables, the snack-bar with a lobster displayed on it, the pretty barmaids and the pewter tankards. The Saloon Bar is comfort, elegance and the feeling of doing well yourself; and very pleasant that feeling can be."
Small beer	A weak beer, usually the result of a second brew from the original ingredients, drunk at home, particularly by women and children.
Stout	Thickish dark beer with a taste of roasted malt — the national drink of Ireland. Guinness is the best known brand.
Tavern	In medieval and Tudor times it was an alehouse which offered a roof over the head for the night.
Tie	An agreement forcing a pub to sell only the product of a single brewery.
Tied estate	The pubs owned by a brewery.
Tied house	A pub owned by a brewery which normally sells only the brewery's products. The pub is leased to a tenant who pays rent to the brewery out of his takings.

Vaults   A name given to one of the rooms often found in northern pubs. This was the place where women would sit, while their menfolk were in the public bar.

Wet and dry sales   The items sold in pubs are often divided into wet (beers, wines, spirits, etc) and dry (food, cigarettes, etc).

Yeast   A vital ingredient in beer giving flavour and zest to the final product.

Further Reading

Anthony Avis, *The Brewing Industry 1950-1990* (published by the author 1997) A fascinating account of what the brewing industry was like in the 1950s and 1960s.

Norman Barber, *A Century of British Brewers 1890-2004* (3rd, edition, Brewery History Society, 2005). The BHS is also publishing a number of more detailed county guides to breweries, including home-brew pubs. Counties covered so far are Buckinghamshire, Cambridgeshire, Durham, Essex, Leicestershire and Rutland, Northamptonshire, Norfolk, North East England, Oxfordshire, Somerset and South Yorkshire. Buy online at **www.breweryhistory.com.**

Pete Brown, *Man walks into a Pub: a sociable history of beer* (Macmillan, 2003)

Peter Clark, *The English Ale House, 1200-1830* (Longman, 1983)

Martyn Cornell, *Beer: the story of the pint* (Hodder Headline, 2004)

Jeremy Gibson, *Victuallers' Licences* (Family History Partnership, 3rd edition, 2009)

Mark Girouard, *Victorian Pubs* (Studio Vista, 1975)

Brian Glover, *The Prince of Ales* (Sutton Publishing, 1998) on Welsh brewers and breweries

Terry Gourvish and Richard Wilson, *The British Brewing Industry, 1830-1980* (Cambridge University Press, 1984)

Frederick W. Hackwood, *Inns, Ales and Drinking Customs of England* (Bracken Books, 1985, first published in 1909)

Peter Haydon, *The English Pub: A History* (Robert Hale, 1994). Sutton Publishing republished it under the title *Beer and Britannia: An Inebriated History of England in 2001*

Paul Jennings, *The Local: a history of the English Pub* (Tempus, 2007) the best modern history of the public house

Maurice Lovett, *Brewing and Breweries* (Shire Publications, 1981)

Ian Marchant, *The Longest Crawl* (Bloomsbury, 2006) superb account of a tour round Britain's pubs

Peter Mathias, *The Brewing Industry, 1700-1830* (Cambridge University Press, 1959)

Barrie Pepper, *The Landlord's Tale* (CAMRA, 2006) life in a Yorkshire pub in the 1950s

Lesley Richmond and Alison Turton (eds), The Brewing Industry: *A Guide to Historical Records* (Manchester University Press, 1990)

Hugh Rock, *Pub Beer Mugs and Glasses* (Shire Publications, 2006)

Ken Wells, *Travels with Barley: the quest for the perfect beer joint* (Berkeley Books, 2004) an entertaining account of the American beer scene

See also entries for alehouses and inns in David Hey (ed), *The Oxford Companion to Local and Family History* (Oxford University Press, 2nd edition, 2008) and sections in Andrew Barr, *Drink: A Social History* (Pimlico, 1995).

In addition, occasional articles have appeared in the family history press. In *Family History Monthly* (issues 34 and 85) there are articles on Publicans, and Brewers and their Records in issue 56. Back copies cost £3.60p each (2009 price) and can be obtained from Family History Monthly, 140 Wells Farm Road, London W3 6UG.

A number of local history societies and individuals have published histories of public houses (and less frequently breweries) in their areas, some of which can be very hard to track down. The local studies librarian or archivist should be able to tell you what has been published locally. For some reason Hull is particularly well covered: a list of booklets about pubs in the city can be found at **www.eyorks.com/hullpub/lhu.html**. Copies of books and booklets should have been deposited with the British Library, although this is rarely the case. The Society of Genealogists also has a small collection. A list of publications known to the Pub History Society is at

www.pubhistory.freeserve.co.uk/phs/bib.htm.

Family history societies have been rather slow to publish material about publicans. One exception is Oxfordshire FHS, who published Vera Wood's *The Licensees of the Inns, Taverns and Beerhouses of Banbury* in 1998.

A large variety of books on inns and breweries is sold by Paul Travis, Beer-Inn Print, Long High Top, Heptonstall, Hebden Bridge HX7 7PE, **http://beerinnprint.co.uk**. It is now relatively easy to buy second-hand books online at

www.abebooks.co.uk or **www.alibris.co.uk**.

Websites

The best National Pubs and Breweries website, with a bulletin board and links to other sites around the country is **www.pubhistorysociety.co.uk**. There are also pages about tracing the history of pubs on my web site at **www.sfowler.force9.co.uk**.

There are several sites devoted to pubs of particular counties. The pubs of Gloucestershire can be visited at **www.gloucestershirepubs.co.uk**, and the lost pubs of the Midlands are discussed at **www.midlandspubs.co.uk**. The Potteries Pub Preservation Group is at **www.pppg.supanet.com**, and pages on the pubs and breweries of Bradford are at **www.me.toft.btinternet.co.uk**. For London check out **www.pubs.com/home.cfm**. No doubt there are other sites which also contain material of this kind.

There are also a few sites devoted to inn signs, such as that of the Inn Signs Society at **www.innsignssociety.com**. Darts is an important game played in many pubs and **www.patrickchaplin.com** tells the story of the game.

There is also a mailing list devoted to pubs and publicans: ENG-PUBS-INNS. To subscribe send "subscribe" to eng-pubs-inns-l-request@rootsweb.com (mail mode) or enf-pubs-inns-d-request@rootsweb.com (digest mode).